It's Not My Story

by
Anne K. Pfeffer

It's Not My Story

This is not my story. It's not even my story to tell.

My father was seventeen years old when the world as he knew it came to an end. It ended as he lay on the roof of his home putting out embers and flames so that his house didn't catch fire. It was 1939, and the Germans were bombing the town of Josefov, Poland, and strafing anything that moved on the ground. A lot of people died that night. A lot of houses went up in flames that night, but not my father's house. He later regretted that act of heroism. I remember how sad he looked when he told me that he should have let the house burn. One-half of the Jews of Josefov who were burned out that night and consequently left town, survived the war. Of those who remained in Josefov, almost no one survived. His mother, father, and three sisters all were murdered in the ensuing bloodbath.

I was never told "everything." It is an impossibility to be told "everything," particularly when "everything" encompasses almost seven years. Also, the fact is that some things are too awful and too painful to recount. I was spared a detailed description of the horror so that I wasn't traumatized, and the teller of the tale was able to ease his path – well, maybe just a little. Memories can be intense experiences. Perhaps some memories are best left tucked away beneath a huge emotional and psychological grindstone, or they might rise up to crush us.

There is no one alive today who can correct my mistakes and fill in the gaps. The rightful owner of this tale, the man who lived it, is dead. I had often thought of "debriefing" him. He would speak into a tape recorder, while I posed questions. I hadn't quite worked my way up to asking him to do this because I knew how painful it would be. Then quite suddenly the point became moot. He suffered a terrible brain injury in a fall. The doctors gave him only a 30 percent chance of survival. After two weeks in a coma, he did survive but with damage to his frontal lobes. For him, past and present became a jumble peppered with hallucinations.

My father, Joseph Kalichman, died in December 2002. Most of the stories he recounted to me have a swashbuckling element to them. He could hold his own against Indiana Jones. They are improbable stories of survival based on a combination of guts and luck and daring the absurd. It worked for him somehow. He, however, would only credit blind luck for his survival. He told many of his tales with wry humor or humor of the absurd. The stories seemed so inconceivable, and at the same time I knew them to be absolutely true. My father didn't embellish or exaggerate. He told it as it happened.

A few months ago, my son asked for more detailed information about one of my father's exploits after World War II. I produced an article on that very subject that I had written for an exhibit at the Opalka Gallery of Sage College. After reading the article, my son wanted to know more about his grandfather's extraordinary life and asked me to write down his tales. My son said he was afraid that if I didn't commit the stories to paper, they would be lost forever. He was right, of course. And it's not just my son's wishes that I'm thinking of. My grandchildren should know about the life and times of their great-grandfather.

My father's stories could become a family legacy handed from generation to generation. They are sad stories. They are funny stories. They expose the human condition at its best and its worst. They also give voice to those who died without a voice. I can record on paper the names of family members who died without leaving another written record. In some ways, this written record can serve as an epitaph for those who never had another one.

But memory, as we all know, is faulty. I don't want to make mistakes, although I know I will. And now there is no one left who can correct my errors. I will simply have to do the best I can. At least the broad outlines of the stories will be fairly accurate. Perhaps what is important here is that the tales get told, that they are passed along through the generations. There are important lessons in these tales. They are tales of endurance and of incredible human decency under horrific conditions. This is now my task, and it is a fearful one. To write down my father's tales, I will have to walk in his shoes. For my father, the nightmare was finite. It was the sum of his experiences. For me, since I have no first-hand experiences, the nightmare is infinite. My nightmare is based on what I've heard and read, and I know that my information is but a tiny fragment of what actually transpired.

I have written down what I know of my father's life before, during, and after the war. I understand that what I have written are my memories of what he recounted to me. This record is flawed as to some of the dates and facts, but it is the best I can do.

A shtetl education

My father had a very large family – both immediate and extended. He was one of four children. His father was one of four children who had all married and had children of their own. My father lived in a small town alongside his parents, grandparents, siblings, cousins, close and distant, aunts and uncles. In one way or another, my father was related to almost all of the Jewish inhabitants of Josefov.

Josefov was a shtetl – a small town not too far from the large city of Lublin. Like many such small towns in Poland, the population was heavily Jewish. The population of the Polish countryside seemed to have distributed itself with a large percentage of Jews living in the small towns, and mostly Catholics living on farms and in villages. There were historical reasons for this arrangement. For many centuries in many cultures, Jews were forbidden to own land or to farm rented land. So to earn a living Jews became merchants, shopkeepers, bankers, artisans, and professionals – all trades that usually meant living in town. This is not to say that in 1939, there weren't some Jewish families who farmed or that there were no Catholics living in towns. But mostly, the shtetls were "home" to a predominantly large Jewish population.

Anti-Semitism always roiled close to the surface. If you were Jewish, you were always conscious of it and careful not to "step out of line". Discrimination was rampant. By 1939, Poland offered all of its citizens (including Jews) universal elementary school education through the sixth grade. Further education required payment to attend a secondary school that was called a gymnasium. Jews were not welcome in Polish secondary schools. Of all the Jews in Josefov, only Guta, my father's first cousin, attended a gymnasium. Her father Shai owned the local lumber mill and had the resources to pay for Guta to be admitted to the school. Most people in the countryside, Jews and non-Jews, were too poor to attend secondary school. As soon as they could, children went to work to assist their families in earning a living. Life was a continuous struggle to obtain the bare necessities. If you were Jewish, you had additional hurdles to vault.

The irony of Guta's singular education was that it helped her pass as a non-Jew during the Holocaust. She was so well versed in Polish culture and had even studied the German language in the gymnasium, that she was sent as a "guest worker" to Germany. She had false identity papers to prove that she was a Polish Catholic. Of course the fact that she was a blue-eyed blond didn't hurt either. But mostly I attribute her survival to her education in the gymnasium. The Nazis were efficient at ferreting out Jews who were trying to pass. But Guta had the education to fool them -- and she did.

Dwarf horses and oranges

My father didn't talk much about his life before the war. He would have had to face yet again the immenseness of what had been lost. But on rare occasions he let himself reminisce about a jolly memory – and I was permitted a furtive peek into a long-gone world.

My Grandfather Moshe built the largest private residence in the town. His family inhabited but a small section of the house. The rest was rented out to the local doctor and local dentist and their families. One of the tenants owned two dwarf horses. I remember how my father's face lit up in describing them. He said they were "sooo cute!" Smiling, he shook his head, describing the little cart they pulled and how he chased the horses. My father had such a happy look on his face recalling that memory, but it was a childlike look, and it startled me. It was a rare sight. I think the only other time I saw that look was when he was playing with my one-year-old son. Then my father looked young and fresh and innocent and unhardened by travails – everything he was not. I've often wondered what he would have been like had he not been sent to hell and back.

And then there are the oranges. For years now, I can never eat an orange without thinking what a wondrous fruit it is. I used to consider it commonplace. Not exotic like mangoes because they come from tropical climates. Nothing special like cherries because of a short growing season. Oranges to me were just an ordinary everyday item. That was before my father explained what a precious commodity an orange was in Josefov.

I remember being a child of twelve about to slice open an orange in the kitchen of our apartment in the Bronx. My father walked in just then and broke into a silly smile, telling me that in Josefov, oranges were expensive and hard to obtain. They were also thought to have great medicinal value. Only people who were at death's door, or had one foot out that door, were given oranges to eat. Oh, and they were so pretty to look at. Very few people ever got to taste one, but everyone knew that oranges were scrumptious. I'm sorry now that I didn't ask him when he got to taste his first orange. In many ways my father mirrored other immigrants' appreciation for the opportunities afforded them in this country. I don't think he was ever expecting streets paved with gold. I do think that he was astounded at the bounty of oranges in the supermarkets – and that he could have one whenever he wanted to.

Family relationships

In the summer of 1987, my mother took me on a trip to Israel to "visit the relatives." I was in the throes of a divorce and shell-shocked. Cut loose from my moorings, I was free-floating, trying to glean wisdom wherever I might find it. We visited with my father's Aunt Miriam in Haifa – reputed to be a very wise woman. Miriam was my father's father's sister – my great-aunt and was in her mid-90's. Miriam's advice to me was that I should dress up, apply make-up, go out and have a good time. She said my friends would be delighted and my enemies furious. And I think that was very good advice.

She told me that she and her husband had owned a bakery in Josefov. She chuckled as she recalled my father's childhood antics as he tried to mooch a cookie from her. Apparently, he pleaded in a winsome and clever manner and she always gave in – he got his cookie. Aunt Miriam's face lit up as she enjoyed her memory, and I felt as if a corner of the veil that had descended over Josefov after the war was lifted. I got a peek at a normal life that had its charm before everything was painted black.

Aunt Miriam attested to the fact that my father was rather spoiled, something he would readily admit to. He was the only son. His mother and three sisters, all four females, indulged him. I gathered that his father did not join in this admiring circle of devotees. Moshe was omitted when my father recounted that his mother and sisters spoiled him. Somewhere along the way I developed the notion that my father and his father had a difficult relationship. My father never really spoke about his father.

There was another problematic and important male figure in my father's life before the war. This was his Uncle Shai (short for Yeshayahu, Isaiah in English). Shai was brother to both Moshe and Miriam. It was Shai who owned the lumber mill. Josefov was surrounded by forests, and lumber was one of the main products. Shai had three daughters. Given the time and place, they did not work in the mill. But my father worked for his uncle, first as a lumber jack, cutting down trees himself or supervising those who did. He then earned a promotion and worked inside the mill itself. It was long hours of arduous work. I remember my father telling me in an exasperated voice that after the workday was done, Uncle Shai would make him wait around for hours with nothing to do before he was dismissed and free to go home. My father shrugged his shoulders and told me that sometimes Shai wanted to talk and ask him questions, and sometimes not. I think his uncle kept him at the mill for company. In any case, we'll never know the motivation behind Shai's perplexing behavior.

I cannot remember my father recounting any other information about Shai to me. So I've put Shai and Moshe in the same category vis-à-vis my father, He had a problematic relationship with both of them.

The value of an education

My father attended public school in Josefov through the sixth grade. This was the only secular education he received, that is, if we disregard the single evening of immigrant "night school" he attended as an adult in Manhattan. He simply didn't have time for "night school." After public school classes were over for the day, all the Jewish children attended the heder. The heder was an afternoon Hebrew school. My father, however, preferred the secular subjects. He loved history and math, and he excelled in both. He used to do complicated calculations in his head. I was always in awe of his mathematical skills.

When I was 14 years old, and my father was working in the Albany-Troy area, I remember accompanying my father to a bank in that community. He was applying for a loan to purchase land to be used for the construction of private homes that he hoped to sell. The loan was for a large sum of money. I remember the loan officer running through a set of numbers with my dad. After the loan officer concluded, my father told him that he had made an error and also stated what the correct amount should be. The loan officer argued that he had checked his figures with a calculator and produced the tape – this was clearly before the days of computers. My father insisted that there was an error and that the loan officer needed to re-check his calculations. The loan officer complied and, sure enough, found the error. He was amazed and asked my father how he knew that an error had been made, and my father answered that he had done the calculations in his head. He never put pencil to paper to do mathematical calculations until he was in his 70's -- and then only ruefully.

My father was a top student in school in all of his subjects except for one – penmanship.
Penmanship was an important subject and my father was abysmal at it. But it was hardly his fault. He was left-handed. In Poland when he was in school, you were not permitted to write with your left hand. Forced to write with his weak hand, he did so very poorly all through his life. He would lead with his left hand to perform other tasks. I think forcing him at an early age to use his weaker hand in a manner unnatural to him, confused the development of dexterity in both hands. My father was useless in fixing or repairing things. His brain would tell him what to do, but his hands just couldn't do it. He was very good at directing, but lacked the dexterity or finesse in his hands to do the work himself.

At twelve years of age, I was sent to a business school to learn how to type. My father needed to have papers typed, so I became his secretary. He told me to "always learn everything you possibly can, because you never know when some knowledge will be useful." Even at that age I knew that during the war some people survived because they had skills that were needed by someone and so they were spared. You never know.

The nightmare begins

I don't remember the exact circumstances that evoked my father's vivid recollection. I believe we were sitting in our living room in the apartment in the Bronx and I was in high school. Clearly, the conversation must have involved the past in some fashion, because my father recounted a rather bizarre and chilling tale that occurred a few months before the start of World War II. He told the story to me only once, and so my information is very sketchy, but the imagery was so vivid I never forgot it. It was a portent of the nightmarish things to come.

There was an old woman who lived in Josefov who made her living by supplying fresh milk to the residents of the town. On a daily basis she rose very early in the morning and trekked out to the local dairy farms. There she would purchase fresh milk that she would then haul back to town to sell to her customers. I remember my father sighing, shaking his head and muttering "Oy, yoy, yoy," as he must have seen her in his mind's eye. He called her by name and I can't recall what that was, but I do remember that it ended in "le," which turns the name into an affectionate diminutive. I've decided to call her "Chavele" for the purpose of this story. I remember asking a technical question. How did she haul the milk back to town, -- did she have a wagon pulled by horses? My father looked shocked and surprised. "Horses, wagons? She was a poor woman," said my father. I'm surmising now that she must have had some kind of handcart that she either pushed or pulled by herself on her daily rounds.

One early morning a few months before the start of the war, Chavele was returning to town from the dairies with her milk supply. The dawn was breaking, it was very quiet and no one else was in sight. She happened to glance skyward, and there clearly outlined against the still dark sky was a bloody broom. Chavele ran to town in a panic, and I don't know who she informed, but soon the whole town knew of her vision. No one ridiculed her, or dismissed her tale as a bit of daydreaming nonsense, or intimated that she was an old woman who was becoming addled. People were fearful. The times were very fearful, but the appearance of a broom in the sky dripping blood was a very bad omen indeed.

The Germans arrive

In September 1939, the Germans bombed Josefov. There were no targets in the town of military value. Civilians who fled burning buildings were strafed by fighter planes. The Nazis systematically and calculatedly sowed terror in the civilian population. My father, a young man of eighteen years old, climbed up to the roof of his family's house to extinguish any embers or flames that might ignite the wooden roof. In my mind's eye, I picture a scene of utter chaos and destruction. The noise of the airplanes and bombs and explosions and machine-gun fire and people screaming and fires burning must have been overwhelming, and still my father stayed at his vulnerable post and protected his home. The house survived. The family stayed in their home and their fate was sealed.

Shortly thereafter the Soviets arrived. They encouraged the local inhabitants to leave and to head east away from the Germans. In some cases, the Soviets even provided wagons to transport people eastward. People who were burned out by the German blitz and had already lost everything, and those few who determined that they did not want to stay around for the inevitable German occupation left the town and headed east away from the advancing Germans. The Soviets departed, and almost immediately the Nazis arrived.

There were Jews in Josefov who had lived under German occupation during World War I. They assured their compatriots that while living under German occupation wasn't easy, it wasn't horrific either. It was survivable. Of course, their assumptions were based on the behavior of the former German army. They didn't know that the current German army, the Nazi army, was a different beast with a specific all-consuming agenda where Jews were concerned.

My father recounted that at first things weren't too bad. The men were conscripted for work details, and the women and children were not harmed. The conscription of local males to work for the conquering army was an expected event. Thus it had always been throughout history. The local inhabitants assumed that the Nazis would behave in the manner of other conquering armies. They assumed that the norms of war as practiced by civilized societies would prevail. The conquered did not understand that the Nazis created their own norms and justifications. The Nazis proudly upended civilized behavior. The fatal flaw was to try to deal with the Nazis as if they were part of a normal world. Only those who comprehended that the world had gone mad, and were able to adjust their behavior to function in a mad world stood much chance of survival.

The situation deteriorated. Jews from surrounding villages were forcibly removed from their homes and deposited in Josefov where they became the responsibility of Josefov's Jews. This concentration of Jews into one area served multiple purposes for the Nazis. Shifting Jewish populations into new communities where they were strangers greatly reduced the likelihood that the non-Jewish population might aid these people. Also with food, shelter, clothing and medicine in short supply, epidemics broke out and people started dying – part of the Nazi plan and cheaper than killing them by other means. Lastly but most importantly, since the Jews were already concentrated in one area it would simplify the killing process once the order was issued.

Daily life became a constant struggle to find food. People started dying from starvation. There were railroad lines running near Josefov. The inhabitants saw the cattle cars rolling by filled with people. My father said that the local Jews knew where the people in the cattle cars were going, but rationalized the events by stating that the people in the cattle cars were not "good workers." In other words, if you were a "good worker," the Nazis would not ship you away to what was surely a dire fate. Clearly the Germans required much work to be performed, and if you were a "good worker," they needed you to perform that work. It was illogical to think otherwise, or so people said and thought.

I often wonder how many lives were lost needlessly to such thinking. If only the Jews had realized early on that the Nazi goal was to obliterate them, perhaps more could have been saved. But that was very difficult concept to wrap your mind around at that time in the 20th Century. As my father recounted his tale, time and time again in spite of evidence to the contrary, his thinking was still caught in normative patterns and he suffered greatly for these errors.

The summer of 1942 – the situation is dire

By the summer of 1942, the Jews in Josefov were in an extreme state. Starvation, epidemics and random roundups and shootings were rampant. The Nazis had approved their plan for the Jews, the Final Solution, and mass killing would come to Josefov.

One day somewhere outside the town, my father was captured by a local Polish ruffian named Broz Something-or-Other. I don't recall the rest of his name, and I don't remember if Broz was his first or last name or part of either name. My father offered no further information about the circumstances of his capture, such as where it happened and why he was captured. I do recall that he laughed when he mentioned Broz's name. He said that Broz was the biggest gangster in the area who came from a long line of gangsters spanning many generations.

Broz told my father that he was going to kill him. My father in disbelief said something like, "You're not going to kill me. Why do you want to kill me? I haven't done anything to you." At that point, Broz recognized who my father was. My father was the grandson of Pinchas, a very charitable and kind-hearted man. Soft-spoken and gentle Pinchas took pity on Broz's impoverished sister and her family. He would collect clothing that his grandchildren had outgrown and deliver them to Broz's sister's family who lived deep in the woods on the outskirts of town. Broz informed my father that based on the merits of Pinchas, he was freeing my father. He also told my father to run away because if he caught my father a second time, he would then kill him. Pinchas's kindness to Broz's sister bought my father one free pass from Broz. My father recounted that he was still in disbelief, and asked Broz why he wanted to kill him? The answer Broz gave him was that the Nazis were paying five pounds of sugar to anyone who killed a Jew and brought the body to them.

I seem to recall that I was told this story only once, when I was in my early teens. Many years later, as an adult of forty, when visiting my father's Aunt Miriam in Israel, I learned of the rest of the Broz episode, which my father would not, or probably could not, speak of. Broz and his henchmen had captured a number of Jewish males along with my father. He let my father go, but he and his gang hanged the rest. One of those hanged was the boyfriend or fiancée of my father's sister Leah.

Pinchas's fate remains a mystery. He left the family home one day in search of food somewhere, anywhere, and never came home. No one ever saw him again. My father and his father Moishe took to hiding in the woods surrounding Josefov during the week and coming home for the Sabbath. His mother and three sisters remained in the family home. At this point, people still thought that the Nazis were hunting only for the men and that the women and children would be safe. It cleaves my heart to think that the pull of tradition and civilized behavior was so strong that my father and grandfather would leave the safety of the woods to be with their family over the Sabbath. They risked so much for some semblance of normality.

The murders and incarceration

My father and his father, left their hiding place in the forest and went home for the Sabbath as per their new routine. Monday morning as usual, they were supposed to return to the forest. My father recounted that he didn't know why, but he told his father to go ahead without him. He told Moshe that he would join him a bit later, that he wanted to stay home a little longer. I of course, wonder if he didn't have some kind of premonition that something terrible was about to happen and he wanted to be there to protect the womenfolk.

My father didn't know why on that particular day he opted to stay behind. It was July 13, 1942, the day that his mother and three sisters would die along with 1,500-2,000 Jewish women and children from the town of Josefov. My father never described the scene to me as the Nazis captured him and his family. I can only assume that it was too painful for him to recount the events. I did learn from Aunt Miriam that his mother and three sisters were hiding from the Nazis in a potato field behind their house. They were seeking cover amidst the potato vines. A neighbor informed on them. He told the Nazi soldiers where to find them. Miriam also told me that Leah, the eldest daughter, was a very brave girl. When she was captured by the Nazis, she took off her shoe and threw it at one of the Nazi solders. It took a lot of courage to do that. I don't know if she was punished immediately for that transgression. Aunt Miriam explained that Leah was showing her disdain for the Nazis with the only means she had available to her. At that point, Leah knew she was going to her death. I surmise that my father must have guessed what was to follow. He was always a courageous man of action. To be utterly helpless to protect his mother and sisters from impending doom must have been horrendous for him.

My father recounted that the women and children were separated from the men. The women and children were taken to the forest outside the town and shot, and their bodies dumped into a mass grave. The men were taken to the "lager" – the camp. The method of transporting the men to the camp was something my father vividly described. At the local railroad station the men were to board cattle cars that were bound for the camp. I don't recall how many kilometers my father said separated the town from the railroad station. The Nazis in their unbridled sadism found yet other means of torturing their captives. They forced the men to run to the train station.

The Nazis were on horseback and the Jewish men were forced to run before them all the way to the train station. Any man who stumbled or fell was shot. It was a very hot summer day. When the survivors arrived at the train station they were given extremely cold water to drink. A number of men went into convulsions and died. Those remaining alive were loaded into cattle cars to travel to the work camp. The trip took three full days and nights. They were given no food or water. It was stifling hot in the car. There wasn't enough air to breath. My father helped create a hole near the top of his car to let in some air. He told me that he considered jumping out through that hole but decided not to. Perhaps he reasoned that jumping from a moving train was problematic enough. Who knew if he would survive the fall? And where would he go? Who would help him? He was prey to everyone and hunted by everyone.

After three days and nights in transit, the cattle car arrived at the work camp my father called Lipowej 7. When the doors of the car opened half the people were DOA – dead on arrival. In May 2011, I went on a trip sponsored by my synagogue, Beth Tfiloh, to some Eastern European cities. We also visited a few concentration camps including Majdanek, the concentration camp where my father was imprisoned. At the Majdanek Museum, I learned that the work camp which had been nearby, is referred to as the camp at No. 7 Lipowa Street. References to this work camp in English use the name Lipowa, though the Polish name would be Lipowej.

I asked the tour leader if we could go there. I was told that we were on a tight schedule, but that the bus would drive by the site. I was left dumbfounded as the bus drove right into the heart of the city of Lublin. Today, there is a modern mall with movie theatres where the camp once stood. There is a small plaque affixed to the outside wall of the mall which I could see as we drove by. The plaque commemorates the site of the work camp – at No. 7 Lipowej Street—where my father and others suffered terribly. I was aghast that this nefarious place was apparently during the war part of the city of Lublin. And the reason why there is a plaque commemorating this dreadful place can only be described in bewitched terms. Our local guide explained that in many locations in Poland – after the war of course—when people tried to build on sites that were formerly of Jewish significance the builders ran into all kinds of bizarre construction issues. Weird things happened. They discovered that if a plaque was affixed to the structure commemorating what had previously stood on that site, then construction could continue and the structure could be completed. I suppose the "spirits" of the dead needed to be appeased.

Life in the work camp

Almost immediately upon arrival at the camp, the men of Josefov were treated to a dental procedure. I use the term with much sarcasm. My father and the other men with him had their molar teeth yanked out. Of course, the Nazis didn't bother using anesthetics. The point was to inflict maximum pain. The men were told by the camp guards that their teeth were removed so that they would not eat too much – not a likely prospect in any event. It's quite amazing how creative the Nazis were in giving vent to their unbridled sadism.

Shortly after his arrival at Lipowej 7, when he was still new to the mores of camp life, my father made a terrible mistake that almost cost him his life. A German asked the new arrivals for volunteers. He needed good workers, who would then receive better treatment. My father and other men with him volunteered. The "volunteers" were taken to a special area under guard. One by one they were stripped of their shirts, tied to a whipping post and lashed with a cat o'nine tails. Legendary German ingenuity had extended to improvements of this cat's bite. There were lead weights attached to the ends of each tail of the whip. Not only did this cat o'nine tails slice the men's backs, but it also left holes. I once asked my father about the scars on his back. The skin had healed, but was puckered around round holes. And this was the explanation I received.

One by one every man was beaten. They all had to stand silently watching and waiting for their turn. The silence extended even to the man who was being tortured. If he cried out in pain, more punishment was meted out. By the time it was my father's turn, the Nazi had grown tired of inflicting the beatings. He turned the cat o'nine tails over to the kapo (a prisoner who worked for the Nazis in exchange for better treatment) and ordered him to continue beating the remaining prisoners. Every lash that fell on a prisoner's back was counted. I don't remember how many lashes each prisoner was to receive. But my father did not receive the full complement. The kapo lashing him skipped numbers – and thus spared his life. This particular kapo risked his own life to mitigate the pain inflicted on the prisoners he was ordered to whip. Of those who received the full designated allotment of lashes, many died. My father said that the survivors spent the night "crying like babies." I think that was a telling comment. The Nazi regimen was also designed to infantilize their captives. The object was to break the prisoners' spirits as well as their bodies – making their deaths easier for the perpetrators to effect. And the German who asked for the volunteers stopped by to announce to his victims, "This is what we do to good workers."

I know that the work the men had to do in Lipowej 7 involved construction of some kind, though I don't know if the work was intended to build something useful or merely designed to work the prisoners to death. My father described moving heavy wheelbarrows laden with cement over narrow wooden planks. If a prisoner lost control of a wheelbarrow and the cement spilled out, that was cause for at minimum an intense and immediate beating.

There was one guard in particular that the prisoners feared. In a camp laden with vicious and sadistic guards, this one stood out by the ferocity of his behavior. He was a redhead and the prisoners referred to him as "der Roiter," which simply means the red one in Yiddish. When he was about, the prisoners would whisper to each other, "der Roiter gaite" – the redhead cometh. Everyone was alerted. The object was to keep your head down and somehow make yourself invisible – an impossible task. On his rounds "der Roiter" would randomly fix on a prisoner and beat him severely.

In addition to "der Roiter" making his rounds, another time of high anxiety for the prisoners was the daily "appeal." We would call this a sort of roll call. In the early hours of the morning, the men assembled to be counted. The Nazis added their own special twist on this procedure. Every appeal involved some men being hanged or beaten before their fellow prisoners' eyes. This was done sometimes because of a stated infraction -- and sometimes just because. One day a few men tried to hide during the appeal so as not to be victimized that day. They were discovered hiding. They were all thrown into a shed used for drying wood. The temperatures in that shed were high. They all died, and their bodies were a terrible sight to behold.

At night the prisoners returned to their bunks. They slept on wooden planks nailed one above the other about three or four high. There were latrines outside the bunks. I don't know how far away they were. But my father recounted that all night long urine washed over the men in the lower bunks. He said that the men couldn't seem to control their bladders at night. Having been stripped of all control over their lives, it seems that the prisoners lost control of their bodies as well.

Majdanek—a slave labor/death camp

After a three-month stay at Lipowej 7, the Nazis ordered the transport of 5,000 men and boys from the ostensible work camp to Majdanek, a slave labor and death camp. My father recalled that he weighed eighty pounds at that time. The distance from one camp to the other was not very great. As I stood on the grounds of Majdanek in 2011, I was shocked at how close this camp was to the city of Lublin, and that the site of the work camp is part of the city proper.

Majdanek contained the gas chambers. These men and boys were being sent to their deaths. My father recounted that the gas chambers in Majdanek were placed on the outskirts of the camp, away from the central part of the camp. Indeed on my visit to the camp in 2011, after touring the main area, my tour group was directed to board our bus so that we could be driven to the site of the gas chambers. Four thousand men and boys from the work camp, were sent to their deaths as quickly as possible upon arrival at Majdanek. There were so many to be "processed" that the task could not be completed that day. One thousand men and boys remained alive overnight. They were to go to their deaths the next morning.

My father was amongst this latter group. Milling about the outdoor area near the gas chambers where the remaining men and boys from the work camp were confined, my father noticed that supplies were being brought into Majdanek via a nearby portal in the wall surrounding the camp. He reasoned that the portal led outside the death camp. This was a possible escape route, his only chance of escaping sure death tomorrow morning. My father was busy surveying the situation to plan his breakout, when he was approached by a rabbi who was also part of the remaining one thousand.

I can't name the rabbi. I don't think my father knew his name. What then followed was an exchange between them, which I found to be incredible the one time I was told the story. The rabbi had been watching my father and surmised what he was thinking. He then tried to talk my father out of making a break for it. I remember asking my father in amazement why the rabbi tried to talk him out of taking a chance on saving his life – after all tomorrow would bring sure death. The answer I received was that perhaps the rabbi wanted to spare him further travail. The gas chambers provided an easy death. The odds of survival outside the camp were not good. There was snow on the ground, and my father was barefoot and wearing a striped cotton prisoner's garb. He was emaciated. Even if my father escaped the camp, everyone who saw him would know that he was an escapee, and no one would help him. He was a target for anyone, and he might suffer a far worse fate than being gassed. Clearly my father was speculating, but he felt that the rabbi was motivated by kindness. My father told the rabbi "I want to live one more day." And then he made his break-out attempt.

My father ran out the portal -- which did lead to the outside. Once outside, he was confronted by a dilemma. He was faced with a stream he would have to cross in order to run to the safety of the distant woods. There was a one-lane bridge over the stream. A lone sentry with a rifle guarded the bridge. My father opted to try to ford the stream. When the water level reached his chin, he had no choice but to exit the water – my father never learned to swim. The only option left was to run across the bridge. The sentry didn't shoot. My father ran right by the sentry, and the sentry didn't try to stop him. I asked my father why he thought the sentry didn't shoot him. He answered that perhaps the sentry thought my father was a dead man anyway, and didn't want to be the one who killed him. And then my father added, "You know, they weren't all terrible. If they were, none of us would have survived."

My father dashed to the safety of the woods. Two men and a boy of about ten followed suit and also made it to the woods safely. I don't know who they were or what became of them. The alarm was sounded, and patrols on horseback with packs of dogs were dispatched to hunt down the escapees.

On my visit to Majdanek in 2011, I looked for the stream my father tried to ford and for the one-lane bridge over which he escaped. They were nowhere to be seen. I was perplexed. I asked our guide about a body of water that should have been near the camp. She said yes, "three rivers" near the camp were covered over. I think she mistranslated from the Polish to English. Surely you can't cover over three rivers. But streams can be diverted or covered over.

Our guide was something of an enigma. My tour group had been told that she was not a professional guide but had volunteered to guide Jewish groups through Majdanek. She was soft-spoken and reserved and tried very hard to be helpful. When I told her that my father had escaped from the camp, her face recorded a momentary flicker of surprise and then immediately recomposed itself. I wanted to ask her about her personal background, but I felt that I would be trespassing, so I didn't. I had the sense that guiding Jewish groups through Majdanek was her way of doing penance. I don't know for what or for whom – she was born after the war.

Running and hiding and making his way back home

My father is now alone in the woods being pursued by Nazis on horseback. He's running as fast as he can, but of course the soldiers are overtaking him. He runs straight ahead and directly into a clearing in the woods. He can't backtrack because the Nazis are behind him and gaining, so he has no choice but to run across the clearing as fast as he can to the safety of the woods on the other side. The sound of a rifle shot reverberates through the clearing, and my father collapses. Sometime later (he didn't know how much later) he came to, and remembered the sound of the shot and thought he was dead. But then he realized that he was cold, and wet and hungry – possibly he was still alive. So, he pinched himself to confirm the fact.

The Nazis were gone. He was alone in the woods. He surmised that his dash across the clearing gave the Nazi marksman an unobstructed opportunity to shoot at him. My father heard the shot and dropped from exhaustion. The timing must have been so well synchronized that the Nazis thought they had killed him. Usually such patrols would collect the bodies of their victims. This time apparently they made no attempt to collect the body. My father was alive and free to continue on his way.

The immediate quandary he faced was where to go? He was a hunted man with a price on his head and fair prey to everyone. My father decided to head back home, to Josefov. Home meant people he knew, who knew him and might help him. Somewhere in the woods surrounding Josefov, he hoped to find his father still alive. It is approximately 150 kilometers from Majdanek to Josefov. The journey itself was quite remarkable, and against all odds, it ended in success.

It must have been sometime in November when my father escaped from Majdanek. There was snow on the ground. He was barefooted, wearing a prisoner's uniform and weighed about eighty pounds. Wandering through the woods, he came upon a lone house situated on the edge of the woods. He could not remain outside overnight. He would die from cold or starvation. With no idea of whom the inhabitants were, he knocked on the door and asked for help.

A young girl of about sixteen opened the door and told him to come in. I don't know her name. She was Jewish. The Nazis in a raid had taken her parents while she was out of the house. She expected the Nazis to come back shortly for her too. The first thing she did was to provide my father with dry warm clothing and shoes to change into. The clothes and shoes had belonged to her father. She then cooked a potato soup -- something warm and filling for him to eat. There wasn't much food in the house, but she didn't stint with what there was.

He spent the night in the house. In the early morning he prepared to leave and continue on his journey. He tried to talk the young girl into going with him. He tried to reason with her. She knew the Nazis would come back for her, so why wait for them? Isn't it better to take a chance and try to escape with him than to wait in her house for certain capture? But the young girl said no. The Nazis had taken her parents, and they might as well take her to that same fate. In effect, she had given up. He left alone on his way, and she remained in that house. He never knew what befell her, but he assumed that she must have been killed. I remember the wistful look on his face when he told me this part of his story. I think he always deeply regretted that he could not repay her kindness by saving her from herself. He could not convince her to go with him and take a chance on survival. Of course, the option my father offered was fraught with danger and suffering. He was a fugitive, hiding in the woods, with no shelter and no food, and it was winter. The odds of survival were not good, but there was a chance. She wouldn't take it.

I don't know many other details of my father's journey back to Josefov. I think it took several weeks. He did tell me that he was passed along from one Jewish partisan group hiding in the forests to another one. The partisans supplied him with some food and assistance along his way. More remarkable yet was that sometimes he was integrated into a Jewish work party under Nazi soldier supervision. I was astounded and asked if the soldiers had not noticed a new face in the group who wasn't supposed to be there? The answer was clearly not. My father would slip into the group from the forest, receive some food, and then melt back into the woods to continue on his way. The brave men of the work party risked their lives, if not worse, to help a stranger. Eventually, my father arrived in the environs of Josefov – home.

Reuniting with his father in the woods

My father made it back to the woods surrounding Josefov, to the Jewish partisans hiding there, to his father, Moshe. He never spoke of their reunion. After all he had been through, I imagine when they met the emotional shock must have been stunning. It must have been more so for my grandfather. Moshe knew that his wife and three daughters were dead, and the Nazis had captured his son. The chances of his son surviving and escaping and turning up in the partisan camp were nil. Yet here he was. I remember asking my father about the reunion. He turned away from me, looked down, shook his head and said ruefully that it didn't last very long.

The partisans had burrowed underground in the woods for shelter and most importantly to create hideouts. These hideouts must have been cleverly constructed because my father recounted that at times Nazi patrols were directly above him and yet didn't detect the partisans hiding below the forest floor. The partisans had to leave their tunnels and the forest to search for food. Because there was snow on the ground, the Nazis merely followed the footprints left in the snow by the fugitives and hunted them down.

On the morning of February 7, 1943, the Germans attacked the partisan camp. My grandfather was killed in the raid. When the attack was launched, the partisans scattered and ran away from the

Nazis as speedily as they could. Moshe couldn't run very quickly. He was very arthritic and had been living underground in the forest, in cold and damp conditions exacerbating his arthritis. His feet were so swollen that holes had been cut in his shoes to accommodate the swelling. He just couldn't run away fast enough. I calculate that he was in his forties when he was killed.

The partisans had designated a meeting place some distance from the original campsite for just such an eventuality. If the camp was attacked, the survivors were to make their way to the meeting place, and re-group there. It would also then be determined who had survived and who had perished in the raid. My father made it to the designated spot, but his father never did. He correctly assumed that his father had been killed in the attack.

The perilous conditions did not permit my father to return to the site of the raid. Approximately a year after the attack, he was able to return to the site and search for his father's remains. He found his father's body. I asked my father how he was able to recognize the body after it had been lying exposed to the elements for a whole year. He answered that his father had been wearing a raincoat and he recognized it. My father also said that my grandfather had been saying his morning prayers at the time of the raid. Moshe had been wearing his tefillin (phylacteries) when he was killed, and my father removed them from his body. My father buried his father's remains below a tree in the forest and marked the tree with some kind of symbol. As far as I know, my grandfather's remains lie there below that tree to this day. Moshe's tefillin were damaged and no longer useable for ritual purposes, but my father kept them with him throughout the war. They are now entrusted to me for safekeeping.

Life in the woods

My father didn't recount many details of his life in the woods. He did explain the general living conditions, and he related one or two episodes of significance to him. There were bands of Jews hiding and living in the woods surrounding Josefov. The woods were thick with growth and the fugitives were able to burrow underground and build bunkers that the growth concealed. Some of these bunkers were engineered with remarkable cleverness. Safety was the paramount issue, with comfort taking a far distant role. No fires could be lit at night for warmth or to cook food, for fear that the fires would be spotted by the Nazis or their collaborators. Even in the daytime, it was problematic to build a fire.

After securing a safe hiding place, the next important issue at hand was procuring food. There were Poles who would provide food to the Jews for a price. You had to have money or something of value to barter. There were also some Poles who took pity on the Jews' desperate plight and offered some small help, – but these people were few and often had limited resources of their own. Others were simply too afraid to help even if they were so inclined. The only options left to sustain life were scavenging and stealing whenever possible.

One of the Poles who would provide food to the Jews for a price was instrumental in reuniting my father with his cousin Krainche. Krainche was the youngest daughter of his Uncle Shai. She was eight years old when the Nazis invaded Poland. According to Krainche, her family avoided the roundup and massacre that befell most of the Jews of Josefov in July 1942, by hiding in a bunker which had secretly been built under their house.

Upon exiting the bunker and learning of the fate of the Jews of Josefov, the family was afraid to return to their home and at a loss as to where to go. Krainche further told me that when the Nazis took over her father's lumber mill they installed a man named Koshenovsky (I'm guessing at the spelling) to run the place. This man tried to help them. He took Krainche's family including her two sisters, her parents, and my Great-grandfather Pinchas, to the mill to live and work there. She said it was like living in a camp. Koshenovsky also went into town where Jews who hadn't been massacred were collected by the Nazis. He told the Nazis that if they wanted lumber he needed workers to run the mill. The Nazis sent their captives to work at the mill, and so Koshenovsky succeeded in giving these people a few more months to live.

In September 1942, Judenrein was proclaimed in Josefov, meaning the surviving Jews were to be killed. Krainche was eleven years old. She and her family went into hiding in the woods. By this point, her family was greatly reduced. Pinchas left the "camp" at the mill to search for food and never returned. His fate was unknown. Her eldest sister, Guta, was somewhere in Germany posing as a "Polish" guest worker. Her middle sister Manche had suffered the severance of some fingers on her hand and died in unclear circumstances. Krainche and her parents banded together with another family named Greenberg in the woods. Illness, raids, and starvation took its toll on this group. Shai went out one day looking for food and never returned. His fate is also unknown, a bookend to the fate of his father. There was a final raid, and the little band of survivors desperately ran across a stream to escape their pursuers. Krainche's mother Hinda and the Greenberg children and parents were shot. Only Krainche and the Greenberg uncle survived and reached the safety of the woods beyond the stream. Mr. Greenberg decided that he and Krainche should go to the home of the Pole who provided food to the Jews. The Pole recognized Krainche and guided her to where my father was hiding in the woods. Krainche spent the rest of the war with my father in the woods. I remember him telling me that she suffered more than anyone else during that time. All the others were adults and could help themselves. She was only a child, helpless and dependent.

The people hiding in the woods lived under brutal conditions, but somehow maintained their humanity, sometimes incurring great risks to do so. The burial of Krainche's mother and the Greenberg family is a poignant example of this. Jews are commanded to bury the dead. When Krainche told my father what had befallen her mother and the Greenberg family, my father organized a burial party. In the dead of night, these fugitives went back to the stream which contained the bodies of the victims of the raid. The Nazis had left the bodies in the water. It was winter and the stream had frozen encasing the bodies in ice. The bodies had to be chopped out. They were then buried in the woods. I can only imagine the terror felt by everyone in that burial party. The noise of chopping ice could have alerted anyone in the vicinity, putting their own lives at risk. And yet they persisted and completed their task. The dead were buried in the ground.

Life in the woods was ephemeral. Survival hinged on arbitrary choices and chance. But this following story my father recounted is almost a morality play. Vengeance was swift. In addition to the fugitive Jews, there were also bands of Russian guerrillas hiding in the woods. The Russians operated secretly behind military lines to harass the Germans and often considered the Jews allies in their endeavors. Russian partisans and Jewish partisans were living in the woods and hindering the Nazis whenever possible. This alliance was fraught with danger for the Jewish partisans. The Russians were far better equipped and certainly better fed than the Jews. They also had access to vodka. In spite of the danger such behavior exposed everyone to, it was common for the Russians to get drunk and be in a very "festive" mood. Part of the "festivities" during such a night of drinking was to bait a Jew. Jews who suffered this fate were rarely seen alive again.

One night the Russians had been partying. They were quite drunk. A representative was sent from the Russian partisans to the Jewish partisans to obtain a Jew. The Russian specifically asked for my father. He wanted my father to accompany him to the Russian camp. My father refused to go with the man since he was quite sure what awaited him were horrors and he would not survive. The Russian then threatened the entire Jewish partisan camp. He said he would have the Russian partisans attack the Jews and kill everyone if my father would not accompany him to the Russian camp. My father still refused to go with him. Whereupon a Jewish partisan who was adjacent to my father pulled out his gun and said to my father, "If you don't go with him, I will kill you now." My father still refused. The Jewish partisan took aim and fired at my father, but his gun jammed. The Russian left without my father. The next day there was a Nazi raid. The Jewish partisan who tried to shoot my father was killed in that raid.

The war ends

In 1945, as we all know, the war was over. The Soviets had advanced into Poland as the Nazis retreated. The Jewish partisans came out of the woods. My father recounted that he threw away his rifle and vowed never to pick one up again. I remember wanting to ask him if he ever killed anyone, but I couldn't bring myself to ask that question. It would have evoked too many painful memories for him, and I had learned long ago to tread lightly on such subjects. I surmised that he had, more than once, and that such experiences left indelible marks upon his soul.

After living underground in the woods for years, it took some time to adjust to civilized life in houses. It took months before my father could sleep comfortably in a bed. Mattresses were too soft. He slept on the wood floor in his room for a long time until he gradually trained his body to sleep in a bed. Also, all the windows in his room had to be open. Having lived outdoors for years, he couldn't bear the stuffiness of an enclosed room, and perhaps such a room engendered feelings of entrapment. In any case, the survivors who came out of the woods faced immediate challenges. Some of these were minor, but many were major and required quick adaptations in order to survive. The possibility of imminent death still lurked everywhere.

My mother's family was also from the town of Josefov. In fact my parents had been schoolmates. Her family was one of the lucky ones whose home had burned in an early blitz, and then headed east away from the advancing Nazis. My mother's family consisted of eight people, six children and two parents. They all survived the war. The family headed east into Rumania and then Russia. Rumania went back and forth between Soviet and Nazi occupation, but my mother's family managed to avoid roundups and deportations, and finally reached the relative safety of the Soviet Union. After the war they returned to Poland to Josefov.

It was an extraordinary and even miraculous occurrence to find a family who had all survived the war. So incredible was this fact my mother's youngest brother, my Uncle Louie, recounted, that when the family reached the Displaced Persons camp of Bergen-Belsen, Jews would come from miles around to see his family – an intact family of eight people. Krainche told me that she and my father as well as others who had hidden in the woods would spend many evenings at my mother's family's home. The survivors from the woods who were now bereft of their own families must have been drawn like moths to a flame to my mother's intact family. Here was a mother, father, and six siblings -- what a miracle. How wonderful to be included even as a guest in this household. Here before their eyes was some measure of normality. In due time, my parents married. They then opened a small mom-and-pop grocery store in a small town near Josefov. Unfortunately I don't know the name of the town.

Determining to leave Poland

The war ended with the Soviet army ostensibly in control of Eastern Europe. In reality, the situation was very fluid. There was an almost total collapse of normal society. Civil laws were not obeyed nor were they enforced. My father described the situation as one of total "hefker"—the Hebrew word for uncivilized, lack of order, barbaric and savage. Since people didn't fear being held accountable for their actions, they did as they pleased. Such conditions did not bring out the best in people -- brutality often reigned. So after the war, there were many instances of Jews who had survived the Nazis only to be murdered or chased out of town by their neighbors or local residents – not the Germans.

The prevailing conditions at the end of the war were worrisome, but three events convinced my father that he stood in imminent danger. One day while walking down the street of the new town he was living in, he chanced to encounter a former guard at Lipowej 7, the "work" camp where he had been incarcerated by the Nazis. This former guard said in amazement to my father "You are still alive?" The guard recognized my father and my father recognized the guard, which meant my father could bear witness against the guard for his wartime activities. Reason enough for the guard to murder him. I found it curious that my father did not seek vengeance against this guard. My father answered my query with the comment that after the war most survivors did not attack their oppressors even though they could, and they probably would not have been prosecuted for doing so. After all, their world was in a state of hefker and they would have gotten away with taking revenge. My father said he didn't know why most survivors didn't kill those who had killed their families, though there were some who did.

On July 4, 1946, in Kielce, Poland, two hundred Jews who had survived the Holocaust were murdered by Poles. It was a pogrom. After the Nazis murdered so many millions of Jews in Poland, the Poles apparently had no intention of treating Jews any differently than they had treated them historically. It was back to business as usual. The postwar massacre in Kielce, coming right after the Holocaust, convinced many Jewish survivors that it would be impossible to stay in Eastern Europe and rebuild their shattered lives there.

There was another issue that weighed heavily on my father. The Soviets were looking for able-bodied young men to draft into their army. My father was in his early twenties and was viewed as a prime candidate. Serving in the Soviet army was not something he intended to do. If the Soviets drafted you, you had no choice but to serve. Better to leave Eastern Europe and elude their grasp.

And there was a fourth factor that entered into my parents' decision to leave Poland. My mother was pregnant with me. Poland was not a good environment in which to raise a Jewish child. So my parents decided to head west, away from the Poles and the Russians. The Soviets had not yet clamped the Iron Curtain around Eastern Europe. Lots of people were moving around. Some people who had been displaced during the war were trying to get back to their homes in Eastern Europe. Some people were heading west away from their former homes in Eastern Europe. Masses of refugees were on the move. It was possible to leave Poland, and so my parents left.

Life in Bergen-Belsen, the Displaced Persons camp in the British zone

My parents headed west out of Poland to the part of Germany that was not under Soviet control. I presume they did so because Germany borders Poland, and that route was the shortest if you wanted to remove yourself from Soviet rule. I was never given an explanation of why they chose Germany, nor a description of what happened to them on that hazardous trip. I only know that they arrived in Germany and ran into someone they knew, a fellow Polish refugee. He took them to his home and fed them a very watered-down potato soup, which was probably the best he had to offer. This man suggested that my parents go to Bergen-Belsen, which now functioned as a Displaced Persons (DP) camp.

After the war, the Allies divided Germany into four zones – the American, French, British and Russian zones. Bergen-Belsen was in the British zone. It became the largest of the DP camps in Europe. During the war it had been an infamous concentration camp. Upon liberation, the inmates' barracks were burned because they were so infested with vermin and disease. The liberated prisoners were then housed in what had been the Nazi guards' quarters. In addition to the liberated prisoners of the concentration camps, there was a steady stream of refugees, Jews as well as non-Jews, out of Eastern Europe heading west away from Soviet control, who also needed to be housed temporarily. DP camps sprang up all over Europe. My parents' friend advised them to go to Bergen-Belsen where they would receive aid. And so they did. They were later joined there by various survivors of their extended families.

In Bergen-Belsen my parents were given a room on the ground floor of what had been a soldiers' barrack. Bathrooms and kitchens were communal. There was a functioning hospital, where I was born. At its height, Bergen-Belsen housed approximately 12,000 refugees. The Jews set up communal structures – there were schools, newspapers, synagogues and other organizations. A committee to govern the community was created, colloquially called the Komitet. Bergen-Belsen functioned almost as a small-town would, except that it was not independent. The British ruled and had final say on all matters. Sometimes they didn't rule kindly or wisely. Mostly though they left "internal" Jewish community matters to the Komitet, and exerted British control over "external" matters.

Relief organizations –both Jewish and non-Jewish-- provided food, clothing and other necessities but in scarce amounts. Basically, the refugees and those former prisoners who had recuperated sufficiently had to find a way to support themselves. Those who could practice their pre-war professions or trades proceeded to do so. I have a set of flatware, settings for twelve, of coin silver manufactured by silversmiths in Bergen-Belsen. Coins were melted down for their silver content and the silversmiths produced the flatware, which they then sold. Teachers had new pupils to teach. Doctors opened practices. Tailors, shoemakers, and other skilled craftspeople resumed their trades, or tried to. But then there were people who could not resume their previous occupations for a variety of reasons, so they developed a new one. Before the war, my father had worked for Uncle Shai who owned the lumber mill. He cut down trees and saw to it that they were processed in the mill. There were no trees to be cut and processed in Bergen-Belsen. My father was a very proud man. He would not accept help from the various aid agencies. So my father as well as others developed a new profession, a new means of making a living; they became smugglers.

What smuggling entailed

Because Germany was divided into four zones, each administered by a different country, the availability of consumer products varied from zone to zone. The smugglers purchased goods where they were obtainable and brought them to areas where they were in short supply. This was done without the approval of the appropriate authorities – it was an illegal activity. These goods were then sold on the black market – also an illegal activity.

The smugglers viewed themselves as business people – merchants trying to make a living and providing a much-needed service. The smuggled goods were typically flour, sugar, coffee, tea, nylon stockings, watches, jewelry and cigarettes. The smugglers also functioned as money-changers. They changed currencies for people, and they moved currencies from one zone to another. This was a profit-making business, or was supposed to be. The authorities took a dim view of such activities. Smugglers apprehended by Western governments were jailed and/or fined. Smugglers apprehended by the Soviets simply disappeared or, if they were lucky, were given a one-way ticket to Siberia.

Goods were transported by individual smugglers in knapsacks they wore on their backs as they crossed borders on foot – in daylight with various ruses – at night hiding from border controls.

Sometimes the smugglers pooled their resources and rented a truck if a great distance was involved – providing of course, they had a sufficient number of people wanting to go to the same place. Renting trucks was an expensive proposition.

This whole enterprise was fraught with danger. The authorities could intercept and punish the smugglers. They could also be robbed or murdered for the merchandise they carried by villains or people who were desperate. The smugglers' activities became madcap adventures, improbable and sometimes impossible. Yet they frequently succeeded against all odds. Their activities took on heroic overtones. And my father loved recounting his share of daring adventures as he plied his trade – that of smuggler. He was animated and triumphant when he recounted how he bested various authorities as he pursued his goals. There was nothing to smile about in re-telling his experiences during the war -- those which he was able to recount. There was only loss and suffering. But after the war he could tell stories of his smuggling days when he performed heroic deeds and bested his adversaries. He came out on top – he won! He smiled and laughed as he recalled these escapades.

The night of the 300-plus watches

My father had a few favorite smuggling adventures that he would recount with great gusto. The story of the 300-plus watches was a little different in that he was a bit sheepish when he told this tale. He was just being a careful consumer and doing his "due diligence," but his actions ended up putting his life in jeopardy. It was only due to bad weather, lax Soviet border guards and blind luck that he survived this misadventure.

My father met with a supplier of watches. The supplier had over 300 watches, which my father planned on purchasing to sell in the Russian zone, where there was a great demand for such items. The plan was to load the watches into his knapsack and cross into the Russian zone at night on foot, through the woods, thereby circumventing the Russian checkpoint.

Now, my father was a careful businessman. Before he purchased items such as watches, he wanted to be sure that they were working. So he wound up each of the watches to be sure that they would run. Clearly he didn't think ahead. He was just checking to be sure that the merchandise he was about to purchase was in good working order. What he didn't consider was that once watches are wound up they will continue to run until they run down. So now he had more than 300 ticking watches which he loaded into his knapsack and put on his back. My father said it sounded like a bomb was about to go off. In spite of the racket emanating from the knapsack, he continued with the plan to circumvent the Russian checkpoint by crossing through the woods at night.

It was raining that night. The ground was slippery. My father fell and broke his arm. He now had a broken arm and a din issuing from his back as he traversed the woods at night. Miraculously, he wasn't caught and he made it to his destination safely. I often wondered if the sounds produced by the rain muffled the sounds produced by the watches. It is also possible that the Russian soldiers did not want to venture out into the rain and so were less diligent in their guard duty on that night. In any case, this particular "mishegas utzach gelungen" – a Yiddish phrase my father often used, which roughly translated means, "this lunacy prevailed."

The night the smugglers towed a Soviet military truck

Smuggling was a profession that required a lot of bravado and a whole lot of moxie, as well as a generous sprinkling of pure luck. You also needed to be able to think quickly to adjust to unpredictable events. These characteristics were always required, and my father's tale of the night he towed a Soviet military truck is a particularly good example of such necessities. He thoroughly enjoyed telling this story. He would laugh and giggle at the improbability of it all and how this endeavor so fraught with danger succeeded.

About twenty-five smugglers chipped in and rented a truck. I do not know what their final destination was, but they did have to cross into the Russian zone. The truck was waiting for them at night outside the locked gates of the Bergen-Belsen camp. The British would lock the gates to Bergen-Belsen at night, supposedly for security reasons, but I think also to inhibit illegal activities such as smuggling. The truck waited in the dark at an appointed place with its headlights off to avoid detection by the British authorities. Stealthily, each smuggler made his way to the truck and boarded. Each man carried a knapsack filled with the goods he planned to sell. The back of the truck where the smugglers sat was covered, probably with canvas, so that no one who viewed the passing truck could see the men and their knapsacks. My father sat up front in the cab with the driver.

When everyone had boarded the truck, it proceeded on its way in the dark with its headlights off until it had cleared the area near the camp. The driver turned on the headlights once he felt he had travelled a sufficient distance from Bergen-Belsen, and the group continued on, uneventfully for a time. Suddenly, as the truck rounded a turn, a Russian patrol flashed bright lights and weapons and forced it to stop. My father immediately whispered to the men in the back of the truck to be absolutely silent.

A Russian soldier approached the truck and explained to my father that his truck carrying Russian soldiers had broken down. My father replied something to the effect of, "No problem, just hook up your truck to the back of mine, and we'll tow you to wherever you want to go." The Russians happily complied. So now my father was sitting in the cab of a truck with some twenty-odd hidden smugglers and their illicit goods towing a Soviet military truck filled with soldiers. There were many Russian checkpoints that the trucks had to pass through that night. Whenever they approached a checkpoint, my father showed the soldiers at the checkpoint that he was towing a Russian military truck and was promptly waved through.

Upon reaching their encampment, the Russian soldiers expressed their gratitude for the tow to my father and the driver with much smiling and back slapping, and verbal thank-yous. The trucks were uncoupled. The smugglers proceeded undisturbed to their destination.

The wonder of it all was that no one checked the rear of the smugglers' truck to see what the truck was carrying – not the Russian soldiers in the broken-down truck nor the soldiers at the various checkpoints. Had the smugglers been discovered, it would have meant dire consequences for them all. My father must have been a master of sangfroid. He could not let on to the Russian soldiers in the disabled truck by his body language or voice that he had anything to hide. He played a jovial, helpful, neighborly sort and gave them a tow to their destination. This ruse played exceedingly well, for not only did the smugglers avoid detection by the soldiers in the truck, but they were also waved through the checkpoints. I can only imagine the terror felt by the smugglers sitting in the back of the truck silently and helplessly as their fate was determined.

The putrid soup and the diamonds

The very nature of smuggling meant that danger was built into each and every endeavor. It's hard to imagine, but a certain degree of riskiness was endemic to every enterprise. So of the many smuggling escapades my father undertook, he only recounted those that stood out above the rest because of an uncommonly high level of danger involved and the improbability of the events that transpired. The rest were deemed too boring and run-of-the-mill to recount.

The putrid soup and the diamonds is such a story. It started out as a "normal" smuggling trip. My parents and some of their friends and fellow smugglers were dispersed within a stream of refugees traveling on foot from one zone to another. Each smuggler traveled alone so that if one was caught by the authorities, the rest would not be nearby and therefore could escape. My father was walking up front and my mother was further back in the flow of humans on the move. A Russian patrol picked my father out of the crowd and brought him to their commander's headquarters. A friend of my parents' saw what befell my father and dropped back into the stream to inform my mother. There was nothing she could do at this point, except to continue onward to her destination to await any further tidings.

My father didn't know why the Russian patrol singled him out. The commander to whom he had been brought decided that my father was a ringleader of smugglers and proceeded to press him for information. My father had a small working knowledge of the Russian language, but he pretended to have none. The commander and my father resorted to pantomime to communicate. Bribery was a common practice and a universal language, so my father proceeded to his next ploy. He rolled up his sleeve to expose an arm covered in watches. He gestured to the commander to help himself to some of the displayed watches. The Russian took some of the watches, but made no move to free my father. Clearly, more inducements were needed. Out of his knapsack, my father produced pairs of nylon stockings – highly desirable items. Once again, the commander accepted the "gifts" but declined to free my father in exchange. The Russian then spied a can in my father's knapsack and reached for it.

At all cost, my father had to prevent the commander from confiscating that can. The secret contents of the can were the reason for this smuggling trip – not the watches nor the nylon stockings. If the contents of the can were discovered, my father faced at worst a quick death or at best a lingering one in Siberia. My father lunged for the can. He grabbed it and a spoon and squatted down on the floor preparing to eat its contents –soup. This can was no ordinary one, it had a false bottom which contained diamonds. When my father pried off the lid of the can and exposed the soup, the room filled with an overpowering stench. This same can filled with the same soup had been crossing borders for weeks and the soup had spoiled and was fetid.

My father, who was dressed in country bumpkin clothes, acted his part to perfection pretending that he would relish eating such a yummy soup. The Russian commander was filled with disgust at the stench and that my father was going to eat the source of that awful stench – the putrid soup. It was more than he could bear. The Russian grabbed my father by the scruff of his neck and the seat of his pants, yanked him outside and kicked him down the stairs of his command post. He then yelled at my father to get lost and added many expletives. And to rid himself of this whole disgusting episode, the Russian commander went back into his office and grabbed the reeking can of soup. He came back outside his command post and threw the can down the stairs squarely aiming at my father. He muttered something in Russian. I wonder if it was the Russian version of bon appetite.

My father took the can and went on his way. I remember that when he recounted this story, my mother was in the room. She became very defensive when he described how badly the soup stank. She took it as a critique of her cooking ability. My mother explained that they had been very busy for weeks crossing borders and smuggling and she simply hadn't had the time to cook up some fresh soup for the can. I think she missed the broader picture. Had the soup not stunk my father and the diamonds would never have been seen again.

The tale of the two suitcases

The authorities were not the only people the smugglers had to be wary of. Since money was involved, one always had to be vigilant that no one spotted their activities. The smugglers were constantly afraid that someone would either inform on them to the authorities, or rob them of their goods or funds. The tale of the two suitcases is a story involving treachery. Who did it and how they did it, has remained a mystery.

My father told me that he and my mother's family had two suitcases that they filled with Deutsche marks, the German currency. They decided to place each suitcase in a separate public locker at either the local bus or train station – I can't remember which it was. I remember asking my father why they did that, but he shrugged his shoulders and laughed and didn't answer. It could be that by the time he told me this story, he had forgotten why he felt the need to place the suitcases in a depot locker. I'm assuming he had a premonition that something was amiss and that the money would be safe under lock and key in a public place and not in his home. And if his home was searched by the authorities, they would not find any incriminating evidence to be used against him.

My two uncles drove the suitcases to the station. They separated once they exited the car, each one taking a suitcase. They entered the depot separately. Each one rented a locker and placed the small suitcase he was carrying inside, locked the door and took the key and departed. The two lockers were not near each other. My uncles met up at the car and drove home. Placing suitcases in lockers is a normal activity for such a facility and should not have aroused any suspicions. That is why my family made use of the depot.

About a week or so later, it was time to retrieve one of the suitcases. Again, my two uncles drove to the station to reclaim it. It didn't matter which suitcase they reclaimed because they both contained nearly identical amounts of Deutsche marks. They randomly chose one, unlocked the locker using the key, extracted the suitcase, returned the key to the depot manager and returned to their car. They placed the suitcase in the back seat of the car and headed home.

After driving a short distance, one of my uncles noticed that there was a German police van gaining on them. They tried to outrun the police van to no avail. So in desperation, they tried to throw the suitcase – the evidence -- out the window, but they didn't succeed partially due to their car's high rate of speed. My uncles were forced to stop their car and were surrounded by German police. The police ordered my uncles out of their car and then extracted the suitcase. The suitcase was opened and everyone present fell silent. Finally, one policeman spoke to my uncles and asked, "Did you shit on us, or did someone shit on you?" For to everyone's amazement, the suitcase contained cut up and rolled up newspapers. My uncles were speechless. They were as surprised as the police. The police clearly expected to find contraband of some kind in the suitcase, or they wouldn't have pursued my uncles. My uncles had expected the suitcase would be filled with Deutsche marks as it was when they placed it in the locker at the depot.

Possessing a suitcase filled with newspapers is not a crime, so the police had to let my uncles go. And home they went to recount the tale. My father wanted to immediately drive to the depot to ascertain what had become of the second suitcase. He was talked out of this action by the family on the grounds that this was probably a trap. They felt that surely someone had informed on them to the authorities. The police most likely were staking out the depot, and when he would retrieve the second suitcase (if it was still in its locker) he would be arrested. In any case, they were sure that the Deutsche marks had been removed from the second suitcase as they had been from the first. They felt my father would be risking his freedom and his life to no avail.

At first my father listened to their admonitions. However, soon the dire circumstances of the family overcame his fear. Basically, the family had lost all its capital. You cannot do business without resources. The money contained in the first suitcase was gone. But what if the second suitcase remained untouched in its locker? It was a slim chance that the money was still in that second suitcase, but he felt he had no choice but to find out. So off he went to check it out.

My father drove to the depot. He had the key and locker number and he proceeded to retrieve the suitcase. He put the suitcase in the car and headed home. No one followed him. Not the police nor anyone else as far as he could tell. When he felt it was safe to do so, he pulled over and opened the suitcase – and it was filled with Deutsche marks, as he had originally packed it. The family had lost half its capital, a blow but not a decisive one. There was enough money left to do business.

I've often pondered this story. I don't know why my father decided to put the family's entire funds in depot lockers. That is a drastic step, and he must have had a strong reason for doing so at the time. I stated earlier that perhaps he had a premonition that something was not quite right and the money would be safer in a public place rather than at home. However, now as I've written this story and reviewed it, I'm wondering if he had suspicions of treachery that fell upon close acquaintances or friends, and that he didn't want to divulge these suspicions to me. He had no proof, and he might have been both embarrassed and saddened by his thoughts.

I now also conjecture that it is possible that someone who worked at the depot was involved, and had access to either a master key or a copy of the key to the locker containing the first suitcase. Any suspect behavior would have been spotted in a public place. Someone must have had a key to open the locker and remove the suitcase in a normal manner. The suitcase was then taken out of the public eye and the money removed. I'm also speculating that the suitcase was filled with rolled up newspapers to simulate the approximate weight and feel of the Deutsche marks that had been removed. It is possible that the suitcase was then replaced in the same locker, so that when my uncles returned to claim it, they would not notice that anything was amiss. They surely wouldn't open the suitcase at the depot. It's also possible that the German police were alerted that my uncles were involved in illegal activities and so pursued them after they left the depot. My guess is that whoever the perpetrator was, he or she wanted to divert attention away from the depot. The fact that the police were now involved meant that my uncles would be too afraid to return to the depot to investigate the situation on their own.

The larger questions, of course, are who told the depot employee what was in the suitcase and how did they obtain this information.

I have no answers to these questions. It was with great luck that when my uncles were sent to retrieve one suitcase, they just happened to choose the one that contained newspapers. Had they chosen the other one, the one that still contained the Deutsche marks, the police would have arrested them. My father had no idea why the second suitcase was not also pilfered. And so this episode remains a mystery.

Retrieving hundreds of Torah scrolls

Life in postwar Germany for the refugees was a bit of a free-for-all. The authorities were to be avoided at all cost, if possible. The preferred method of dealing with problems or issues that occurred was to handle the situation yourself. Sometimes these "situations" were not of a personal nature but actually of a communal one. Nevertheless, some people felt a personal responsibility to act on behalf of the Jewish community at large. The story of the rescued Torah scrolls is an example of such actions.

This event took place sometime between May 1948, when the state of Israel was born, and December 1949, when my family and I immigrated to the United States. I don't have the exact date. Sometime during this time period, my father heard a rumor that hundreds of Torah scrolls had been sequestered during the war in a church in Schwerin, Germany, and were still there. He decided to investigate and found the rumor to be true.

The city of Schwerin was the district capital of an eastern area of Germany. The Torah scrolls had been collected from all of the towns in the surrounding area during the Nazi regime. They were hidden in a church basement and so escaped destruction. I don't know how all of this came to pass. I don't know if the Nazis got incredibly sloppy and let these Torah scrolls slip through their fingers – something hard to imagine or somehow miraculous fate intervened. In any case, the Torahs were hidden and protected by the elderly cleric of the church. I asked my father if the cleric was a Catholic priest or a Protestant minister. My father said he didn't know. Having been born and bred in Poland, my father only experienced Catholic clergy, and he might not have been aware of the difference. In any case, it really doesn't matter. This minister or priest risked his life to save these Torah scrolls from the hands of the Nazis.

My father had taken my Uncle Harry with him on the expedition to Schwerin. They profusely thanked the elderly cleric for rescuing the Torahs and then requested that the scrolls be turned over to them. My father and uncle explained that they would remove the Torahs from the basement, load them into their truck and return them to the Jewish community. They also offered the cleric tangible expressions of their gratitude in the form of the currency of the day: nylon stockings, cigarettes, watches etc. The cleric was having none of it. He refused to permit the removal of the Torah scrolls from the basement of the church. I remember asking my father why the cleric would not let the Torahs go? He said he didn't know, but that the cleric was an old man and possibly confused at this point. I wonder if the cleric had risked so much to preserve the Torahs that he couldn't bear for them to leave.

Unable to obtain the elderly cleric's consent to the removal of the Torah scrolls, my father sought out the Soviet district commander since the city of Schwerin was located now in the Soviet zone. After explaining their mission to the commander and offering him some "inducements" for his assistance, the commander accompanied my father and uncle back to the church. The Soviet district commander ordered the cleric to release the Torah scrolls to my father's care. The cleric had no choice but to do so. My father did leave the cleric with some precious gifts to smooth things over somewhat.

Hundreds of Torah scrolls were rescued from the basement of the church. Possibly two to three hundred – my father either didn't count or he forgot the count. All of the Torah scrolls were placed on a boat headed for the new state of Israel, except for a few that made a voyage to the United States. Five Torah scrolls accompanied my father, mother and myself to the United States in December 1949. As far as I know, four of the Torahs reside in a synagogue in Briarwood, Queens, New York. One scroll, the smallest, is housed in a synagogue in Fairfax, Virginia.

Cigarettes and diapers

I was born in the Displaced Persons camp of Bergen-Belsen. When I arrived in the United States I was nearly three years of age. I have no recall of any events that befell me in Europe before coming to the United States. There are, however, certain characteristics that I possess or that have been ascribed to me that can be explained by my experiences in Germany. I admit that these explications are a bit far-fetched, but they are funny and a bit madcap. Since I have no other rationalizations to offer, I will present my conjectures.

I have always been sensitive to the smell of tobacco. Breathing in cigarette smoke or, worse yet, cigar smoke, makes me severely nauseous and my head aches terribly. This reaction caused me severe problems during my college days when smoking was permitted in class and it seemed that almost everyone did. I would suffer nausea and severe headaches for the rest of the day after sitting in a smoke-filled classroom. I always attributed this severe reaction to the fact that I grew up in a non-smoking home and never developed any tolerance for smoke.

There is another possible reason. On one occasion when my parents were recounting tales of their misadventures in Germany after the war, my mother told a story I had not heard before. As I recall, my father was mentioning something about selling cigarettes on the black market. My mother chimed in that one night those cigarettes almost killed me. As the story goes, my father bought a truckload of cigarettes from a wholesaler. This person knew where my parents lived. Without consulting them, he pulled his truck up to my parents' dwelling, opened the nearest window and started tossing cigarette cartons into the room above the opened window. He had almost unloaded his truck when fortunately my mother walked into the room and started screaming for help. Unbeknownst to the truck-driver, my crib was situated directly below the opened window. I was now buried alive under hundreds of cigarette cartons. The fear of course was that I had suffocated or been crushed. I survived seemingly undamaged, except for my over-reaction to tobacco smoke, for which I now have a plausible explanation.

The next story has to do with toilet training and diapers. My mother always maintained very proudly that I was toilet trained by the time I was one year old. She explained that I didn't like being wet and so would tell her when I had to void. I always thought that she exaggerated this tale, particularly after I had my own children and faced the reality of how difficult toilet training is at even much later ages. One day she casually mentioned that when crossing zones in Germany, my parents would pack my diapers with dollars or Deutsch marks to smuggle them past the guards. A light bulb went off in my head. But, of course, I thought to myself, I must have been toilet trained at a very early age. I'm not stupid! I wouldn't shit on dollars or Deutsche marks! I say this tongue in cheek, but it makes for a funny story. It's quite likely that the money bills were not comfortably packed around my "tush," and if I was wet it would only feel worse. It's possible that I did train myself early to avoid as much discomfort as possible.

Magic

A friend described my father's life as magical. I never thought of it quite that way. Certainly, his adventures and misadventures and the fact that he survived the Holocaust against all odds can be described as magical. But now that I'm viewing his life through this lens, I see that his post-Holocaust life was also filled with improbable, possibly "magical" events.

Two particular instances come to mind. Both episodes took place on the New York State Thruway somewhere between New York City and Albany. I was fourteen or fifteen years old.

In the first instance we were driving from New York City to Albany. My father was driving our station wagon, and my mother, younger sister and myself were passengers. We had just left a rest stop, when my father saw a hitchhiker standing alongside the road. He started to pull over to pick up the young man. It was the 1960s. This young man looked like a very scruffy hippie. I was beside myself. Excitedly, I explained that the TV news had just warned people not to pick up hitchhikers because two women in California had been robbed and then killed by a hitchhiker they had picked up. My father turned around in his seat to face me and said, "You don't know what it's like to have to go somewhere and have no money."

So we picked up this hitchhiker who got into the back seat next to me. I scooted over as far away from him as I could get. This young man didn't say much of anything. He kept to himself. I, of course, was sure that he was about to murder us all. We continued down the road in silence for about ten miles, when something did befall us, though not what I was expecting. We blew a tire.

Fortunately, my father was able to guide the car onto the shoulder of the road without a mishap. When the car came to a stop, the hitchhiker said to my father, "Where is your spare tire? I will change the flat for you." At that point, my opinion of the young man changed. He now looked to me like a guardian angel heaven sent to rescue us. My father couldn't change a flat tire. As I've already explained, he couldn't do much with his hands. If we hadn't picked up this hitchhiker, we would have been sitting by the side of the road for quite some time. The tire was changed, and we all went on our way without further issues.

The second "magical" incident that I vividly recall occurred on the Thruway as we were heading from Albany to New York City. We stopped in the unmanned lane of a tollbooth. My father was throwing the required amount of coins into the basket on the tollbooth, when one quarter failed its mark. He commented that one quarter fell on the ground. I told him to just throw another quarter into the basket. I pointed out that there were cars behind us in line waiting and that we needed to move on. But no, he got out of the car to look for the quarter. The cars behind us started honking, and I was greatly embarrassed by this needless scene. Suddenly he popped back into the car with a triumphant look and a big grin on his face. Not only had he found the errant quarter, but nearby on the ground he also found a twenty dollar bill. "See," he said to me, "if I hadn't dropped the quarter and gone looking for it, I wouldn't have found the twenty dollars." I had no retort. And I remember thinking even then that these things happen only to my father.

The apple trees

My father's Great-aunt Sadie and her husband Sol, who was also related to my father, had immigrated to the United States before World War II. After the war, they went looking for family members who had survived in Europe. They found my family in Bergen-Belsen, and sponsored us so that we too could immigrate to the United States. We arrived in New York Harbor on December 7, 1949, aboard the General J. H. McRae, which was a decommissioned transport ship serving under the auspices of the International Refugee Organization (IRO), a United Nations agency, to transport refugees to the United States.

I once asked my father why he chose to come to the United States instead of Israel. He responded angrily, and I think somewhat defensively, that they had killed his own family, and he was the only one left, and there was fighting in Israel. I understood this to mean that as the sole survivor of his nuclear family, he felt an obligation to live and have children so that his family's line was not erased. Israel in 1949 had just fought a war of survival and was still a very dangerous place. And then there was the fact that after the war he threw away his rifle and vowed never to pick one up again.

One day in a conversation with my mother, I happened to mention the story of the Exodus, the ship containing Jewish refugees that tried to illegally enter Palestine before the creation of the state of Israel. She remarked that we, meaning my father, mother and myself, had actually booked passage on that voyage. Then my father changed his mind, and so I did not sail into history on that ship. I don't doubt that my father would have fought valiantly if attacked. But to willingly place himself and his wife and child in a situation where violence was expected wasn't something he was prepared to do. So he chose to immigrate to the United States which seemed like a safe haven, and not Israel, which was a perilous place.

We lived with Sadie and Sol and their son Marvin, in a one bedroom apartment in the Bronx for three months. My father then found a business to buy, a very small mom-and- pop grocery store on 149th Street and Broadway in Manhattan. We moved to a large apartment on the third floor of an apartment house on 149th Street to be close to their store. It was open seven days a week, initially twenty-four hours a day. Eventually, the store closed for a few hours a day in the early hours of the morning. My father hated the store. He felt it tied him down, and he had plans and ideas for better business opportunities. My mother loved the store. It provided her with a set routine and security. She felt that no matter what happened, she would always have food – after all, she owned a grocery store.

After a number of years of living frugally and saving as much money as they could, my father had enough of a stake to purchase a small brownstone containing three or four apartments. As he accrued more funds, he bought larger apartment buildings. My father was guided in his purchases by Mr. Goodes, an older gentleman who took a kindly interest in him. Mr. Goodes was an experienced landlord and basically taught my father the ropes, as it were. Eventually, when the lease for the store expired, my father sold the stock of the store to other groceries in the area and he closed it. He intended to devote his energies full-time to real estate ventures in New York City and purchased properties in Manhattan, Brooklyn and the Bronx.

While he felt liberated from the shackles of maintaining the grocery store, my father wasn't content to be a landlord either. One of my mother's brothers settled in Montreal, where he learned to be a builder of private homes. Half-way between Montreal and New York City is the Tri-City area of Albany, Troy and Schenectady. The two brothers-in-law became partners in a home construction business. They built over five hundred private homes and a garden apartment complex in the Albany and Troy area. My father just loved being a builder. For him it was an act of positive creation. He would take a field or a stone quarry and turn it into communities that housed people. He planted trees and shrubs and grass and everything grew and looked lovely. My father was immensely proud of what he had created.

One day while driving through the Catskill Mountains on the way to New York City, we passed an apple orchard along the highway. My father remarked that a farmer had offered to sell him a prime piece of land on which to build a subdivision. He went to view the land and found that it contained a beautiful apple orchard but decided not to purchase the land. My father said that he could not cut down those lovely apple trees. I responded that someone else would purchase the land and cut down the trees. My father retorted, "Let someone else do it. I don't have the heart to cut down the beautiful apple trees." I remember thinking at the time, that after personally experiencing some of the worst atrocities ever committed, my father miraculously was able to maintain his humanity. He took pity on the apple trees.

Made in the USA
Lexington, KY
27 March 2015